# HOW TO INCREASE YOUR INCOME ASTRONOMICALLY

In business and career

Efezino Akpotu

©Efezino Akpotu 2022

The moral rights of the author have been asserted.

All rights reserved. No part of this publication

may be reproduced, distributed, or transmitted

in any form or by any means, including

photocopying, recording, or other electronic or

mechanical methods, without the prior written

permission of the publisher, except in the case

of brief quotations embodied in critical reviews

and certain other noncommercial uses

permitted by copyright law. For permission

requests, write to the publisher, addressed

"Attention: Permissions Coordinator," at the

address below:

efeheritage@yahoo.com

## Dedication

To my wife and kids for their love and support

# Table of Content

[Table of Content](#)
- [Chapter 1](#)
  - [Become a problem solver](#)
- [Chapter 2](#)
  - [Look For or Ask for more problems to solve](#)
- [Chapter 3](#)
  - [Be different and Unique](#)
    - [6 Things to Master to Be Different From Others](#)

[5. Keep learning always](#)

[6. Surround yourself with inspiring people](#)
- [Chapter 4](#)
  - [Respect for Authority](#)
- [Chapter 5](#)
  - [Profer solution rather than complain.](#)
- [Chapter 6](#)
  - [Love to serve as you work](#)
- [Chapter 7](#)
  - [Walk with great minds](#)
- [Chapter 8](#)
  - [Increase Capacity](#)
- [Chapter 9](#)
  - [Practical steps to increase your income](#)

**Chapter 1**
Become a problem solver

**Chapter 2**
Look For or Ask for more problems to solve

**Chapter 3**
Be different and Unique

**Chapter 4**
Respect For Authority

**Chapter 5**
Profer solution rather than complain

**Chapter 6**
Love to serve as you work

**Chapter 7**
Walk with great minds

**Chapter 8**
Increase capacity

**Chapter 9**
Practical steps to increase your income

Introduction

Life is all about growth. So also in our income and finances.

To increase your income, you must deliberately take financial growth steps.

Financial growth is an aspect of improving your personal finances and becoming more financially stable.

When you are in the process of improving your finances, there are a few other approaches to your lifestyle that you can implement that will improve your financial position further.

Some Action steps that can ensure your financial growth

1. Setting of life goals.

2. Living within your means.

3. Building a solid cash reserve.

4. Using debt services strategically.

5. Having an organised investment plan.

6. Getting more bang for your buck.

7. Leveraging your employer benefits.

8. Expanding your financial education or knowledge.

9. Looking out for other Streams of income.

10. Making your health a priority.


To stop growing financially is to start groaning in insufficiency


To go higher you must pay the price .

Certain steps can never be wished away.

So if you desire to increase your income whether as an employee or a business person or career person, these fundamental forces must be recognized and observed.

## Chapter 1

Become a problem solver

Problems are a gateway to positive change in an individual's life in society.

Problem solving is the process of achieving a goal by overcoming obstacles, a frequent part of most activities. Problems in need of solutions range from simple personal tasks to complex issues in business and technical fields. Wikipedia.

8-Step Problem Solving Process

Step 1: Define the Problem. What is the problem? ...

Step 2: Clarify the Problem. ...

Step 3: Define the Goals. ...

Step 4: Identify Root Cause of the Problem. ...

Step 5: Develop an Action Plan. ...

Step 6: Execute Action Plan. ...

Step 7: Evaluate the Results. ...

Step 8: Continuously Improve.

Any serious business person knows they are in business for themselves.

One major skillset of an Entrepreneur is problem solving. The bulk must always stop at their desk, so they must know how to move the wheel of progress per time.

Any entrepreneur who isn't a problem solver is already a failure. And can't go far in life and business.

Problem solving as it relates to an employee in order to increase their income

There are 2 types of employees:

a. Those who create problems:

They are careless about their job and their contribution to their job.

They are

Unreliable

unfaithful

They are not proactive and need close supervision

They are time wasters

They also waste company's other resources or use them for personal gains

They are clumsy

Disrespectful

Unorganized

They gossip and more


b. Those who solve problems:

These are proactive, mind-over-matter kinds of people.

They care about their job and want to always make meaningful contributions that lead to advancement and progress.

Such employees are

Always in high demand.

They detect problems and solve them. They have good customer service, they are respectful,

Do not participate in gossip

They can work without supervision. They don't waste company's time or use company's resources for personal gain.

They are timely, resourceful and orderly.


Problem solvers merit increase in pay. And often, they do not ask for a raise. They are spotted out like a goldfish and duly rewarded. Even if their boss is wicked and denies them a raise, that can only be temporary.

## Chapter 2

Look For or Ask for more problems to solve

Make sure you are expert in what you are doing or handling. Whether you are an Entrepreneur or an employee

Entrepreneurs look for problems in society to solve. Every problem or societal challenge is an opportunity for wealth to be generated.

In a society where people walk bare footed is an opportunity for low cost shoes to be sold and money made.

In a country where there is shortage of potable drinking water lies an opportunity for bottled water to be sold.

In a community where there is a refuse disposal problem, also lies an opportunity for a refuse disposal business and constant money to be made.

As an Entrepreneur, look for large scale problems in society to solve. If you can't handle them, source for partnership and get to work to fix such problems and get rewarded with wealth.

As an Entrepreneur, build and have a reputation for excellence and quality finished products or services.

Employees, go to your boss, don't ask for increments first, but ask for more assignments and deliver with excellence and timeliness. See work as an exchange for a reward.

When you are solving problems and the company is not rewarding you. Tell them you want to leave. They will renegotiate with you. No one will want to lose a highly effective and productive employee.

When you are a problem solver, you don't beg for increments.

Chapter 3

Be different and Unique

6 Things to Master to Be Different From Others

**1. Believe in yourself**

Start believing in yourself. Start knowing yourself. Start acting the way your soul tells you and not the people. Start accepting your strengths and your weaknesses. You know yourself better. Master what is good for you and act in that way.

**A simple belief can do wonders in your life.**

You are your own role model. Everything in life is possible if you have a belief in yourself. Believe that you can achieve things regardless of what people say. Act towards your way and be consistent in it. Take a step, take action. Don't just sit and visualise it. Act and don't let fear stop you. Conquer the battles, have faith and have belief on your way to success.

2. **Stop taking advice from people**

Stop now. Nobody knows you better than you. You know everything about yourself. You know your power, strength, flaws, mistakes, everything. You know which steps to take to achieve what you want.

Bits of Advice are easily given but it's hard to act. People give advice from their experience they don't know about yours. So, follow your own advice which will guide you to find your path. Start following your inner voice. You are aware of your instincts. So, follow that.

Have the courage to follow your heart and intuition. Face danger and stand up against odds. Be your own hero. You already know what you want to become rest is all secondary. "Follow your own path, no matter what people say"

**3. Don't think much**

Think about the present. Don't worry about the past and future. Think about what you can do today for the better tomorrow. Take steps for growth.

Deliberate your thoughts but when it's time for action, stop thinking and go on.

Calm your thoughts down. Don't take yourself in a negative direction. It is a death valley for you and you will create a problem for yourself. So, follow your heart. Calm your unnecessary thoughts down and don't take yesterday's burden of your life today. These will pile up your heart and mind with irrelevant thoughts.

Work on your thoughts and overcome them one by one. And do what works for you and what your heart says. I guarantee you, your heart knows the way.

"You don't have to see the whole staircase, just take the first step."

## 4. Don't tell your next step to anyone

Don't utter everything to everyone. Keep some things to yourself. If you want to achieve something great, work in silence.

Take steps in silence. Work on your goals without telling anyone.

When you talk to people about your dreams and goals it will be less likely to achieve those goals because people are there to attack you and change your mind. So it's time to not tell people about your goals until you succeed. If no one knows what you are up to, no one is going to stop you.

The less you reveal about yourself to people the more power you will have and the more you will achieve. So, keep things to yourself and achieve the great heights of success.

Keep your plans, super-secret people, and let your result make noise.

## 5. Keep learning always

Life is a learning process. It's not that you give an examination, get a degree and it's finished. The whole life of yours is a learning process. Every step teaches you something. So, never stop learning. Learn about everything you dream of.

Every day you have a chance to learn something new. So grab every opportunity to learn. Discover something new. Prove yourself. Set goals for the day and achieve it. Learn from the tiniest to huge things. So, learn from every aspect of your life. It can be:

- Taking a different route to work.
- Starting a new language to learn.
- Trying new food.
- Decorating home with DIY.
- Starting reading.
- Learning basic home repairs.
- Organizing your cupboard in a different way.
- Learning how to code.

Learn and rise at every step. Take knowledge and wisdom through learning. Grow, experiment with different things, activate your brain, and rise high. Just move at your own pace but move and never stop.

"The beautiful thing about learning is that nobody can take it away from you."-B.B. King

### 6. Surround yourself with inspiring people

It's very important to surround yourself with genius people. Who has a vision and is working hard to prove it. They will push you towards your ambition. Search the people around you and the social media platforms who are in the same field as you. Start networking with people who have succeeded in your fields.

Talk with them. Interact with them. See how they are doing everything. Learn from their journey. Take positive feedback. Surround yourself with people who make you grow. You're a product of your environment. So, surround yourself with the best and become the best.

Your circle is important. Choose it wisely. Be positive. Trust yourself and achieve happiness and success in your life.

"Surround yourself with those

who only lift you higher."

-Oprah Winfrey

You can't make any difference if you don't dare to make an effort to be different. Be quick and swift in delivering your work. prov 22:29

Solve a problem with a touch of excellence and cheerfulness

1The 5:16

Solve problems others are incapable of solving.

If you are not different you can't make any difference.

## Chapter 4

Respect for Authority

Why is respect for authority important? When individuals and corporate entities respect authority, it promotes social order.

This is important because **it allows society to grow and flourish**.

For example, taxes are used to create social programs and fund government policies. As a result, there are roads, public services and more economic opportunities available for the common good of everyone.

How do you obey and respect authority?

**How to obey the rules of law and authority**

1. Explain the purpose of obeying the laws. Explain to your children why it is important for them to obey the law in their daily lives. ...
2. Be a role model. ...
3. Protest the right way. ...
4. Interact with authorities. ...
5. Ensure discipline at home.

Entrepreneurs respect government policies, laws and statutes. Going against constituted authority is one fast way to fall out of favour, patronage, support and ultimately decrease in revenues.

Everything you respect becomes attracted to you. Everything you detest you repel.

Employees, see your boss as that next step to move up in your organisation. He determines your rise. Walk through the door that leads to your promotion with caution.

If you are working in an organisation and not on good terms with the boss you are not wise.

Who determines your promotion, your colleagues or your boss?

## Chapter 5

Profer solution rather than complain.

Complaining stops creativity and blocks your brain from functioning optimally.

There are two types of people in the world -- the ones who complain and

— those who proffer solutions.

Note: Consumption is for those who don't contribute but complain (products and services) are for those who complain; to buy and pay for. They simply enrich the problem-solvers.

Elon Musk didn't complain about Crude oil prices and OPEC, he simply created an alternative electric car and he is the richest in the world at the moment of writing this book.

Anytime people complain, put your ear down to get their pain points, agony, frustration, desires, wishes and wants. Then profer solution to their challenges.

Financial growth depends on your willingness and capacity to solve problems.

If in your country, people are complaining that things are too expensive. Then it's time for the production of new products that cut the price, alternative and cheaper products to be manufactured. Entrepreneurs are sensitive.

Evey expensive thing has an alternative. Be the one who creates the alternative.

Employees, put down your ears to hear the complaints of your boss, society, your customers and ask yourself "how can I meet the needs of these people". That's how to increase income.

## Chapter 6

Love to serve as you work

"**26** Not so shall it be among you: but whosoever would become great among you shall be your [h]minister; **27** and whosoever would be first among you shall be your [i]servant" ~ Matthew 20:26--27 (The Holy Bible)

Service is the ladder to greatness. Put people, customers first. Don't think of the profit first. Think of how your product or service will serve and solve people's problems and challenges first.

Service to the people first.

Don't start a business to make money as the only goal, but to serve the people first. To make a difference and an impact in the lives of people or society, then income will increase once you satisfy your consumers or customers

## Chapter 7

### Walk with great minds

"Iron sharpeneth iron"

"**23** I assure you *and* most solemnly say to you, whoever says to this mountain, 'Be lifted up and thrown into the sea!' and [f]does not doubt in his heart [in God's unlimited power], but believes that what he says is going to take place, it will be done for him [in accordance with God's will]". ~ Mark 11:23

If you want your income to grow, be careful who you hangout with, what you hear and say.

Poor relationships can cause a decline in income. There are people you mix with and your income will begin to dwindle and decline.

When you are close to someone they will influence you. No association or communication leaves you neutral. It must affect you positively or negatively. Everything you keep hearing controls your life and destiny.

Therefore, by intentional design, get associated with right thinking and progressive people. Carefully choose your circle of friends.

Don't leave that to chance or by Default. Make the right choices.

There are people who will never say any productive thing to improve your mind. Mind what you hear.

Steer clear from gossipers.

Every association has a power in you. Every association will always draw from you or add to you. Subtract from you or add to you. No association leaves a man neutral.

# Chapter 8

## Increase Capacity

Capacity is increased either to meet an actual (immediate) increase in customer demand or an anticipated (future) increase in customer demand. Immediate capacity increases are usually achieved by: Using existing equipment for more time (Adding shifts or overtime) Using someone else's equipment (Outsourcing)

**3 Steps To Increase Capacity**

1. STOP doing only those things you've done before and START doing ONLY those things You MUST and Should Do that move you forward in the direction of accomplishing your goals.

The first step toward success is becoming good at what you know how to do, but once you've mastered what you know, you begin to discover other things you could do. Doing what you've done before increases your efficiency, but it doesn't do much for your capacity. Doing new things leads to innovation and new discoveries, which yields new things that you should be doing—things that likely replace those things you've done before.

2. STOP Doing What is Expected and START Doing What is Unexpected

Let me go ahead and clear this up: what most people never expect is to have their expectations exceeded. What others define as a ceiling, you define as a floor, and then seek to go up from there. Being a leader who gives in to the inertia of the daily routine, the same old same old, may allow you to be efficient but it will never allow you to be effective and increase in capacity. You must push past the minimum and seek to do something beyond what's expected. Show up early. Stay late. Listen well. Praise more. Reward faithfully. Share willingly. In a world where leaders are expected to disappoint, be the leader who delights.

3. STOP Doing Important Things Occasionally and START Doing Important Things Daily

If it's important, it's worth doing. That's the leader's mindset. Yet so often we surrender our time to the urgent or the pressing or the "needed" instead of to what's important. To do what's not important each day yields nothing for you or your leadership; it merely uses up your time. And to do what's important only occasionally doesn't lead to the consistency that compounds into results. You must do what is important daily if you want to achieve expansion in your capacity. Ofcourse, increased capacity brings about increased output, results and rewards.

5 Ways To Increase Capacity

1. Good Systems.

Putting efficient systems in place actually enable team members to get more done than they ever imagined. Systems are like a track that helps a locomotive engine make progress more effectively. We need systems to reach our potential.

2. Growth Mindset

According to Dr. Carol Dweck, people tend to embrace one of two mindsets: a fixed mindset or a growth mindset. If we're not intentional, we drift into a fixed mindset that observes past experiences and says, "I'm just not good at math" or "I just can't dance." A growth mindset drops those restrictions, and adds the word, "yet"—"I'm not good at math, yet." Growth mindsets believe development is possible whatever our age.

3. Expanding & Demanding Experiences.

Generally speaking, we do not increase our capacity unless we're placed in demanding situations.

The truth is, people are like rubber bands: we're most useful when we're stretched. Demanding experiences are like lifting weights. They make us stronger. I am speaking of the contexts that force us to work long and hard and show grit.

## 4. Input and Feedback

I learn best when I welcome feedback and develop thick enough skin to take it to heart. I grow the most, not when all goes well, but when life is tough—and I must discover my weaknesses or flaws. John Maxwell often says: "Sometimes you win, and sometimes you learn". My capacity is increased when I invite difficult input into my life. This means I must ask for accountability and assume responsibility for my growth

5. Taking Risks in New Territory. It's very important to recognize that you cannot expand your capacity by continuing to repeat the same tasks and perform the same routines that you had accomplished in the past. The only way you could get to the next level is to progress into new territory. You have to try new things. It's scary but worth it each time you do. Start growing leaders as well.

Increase your capacity

**"Parable of the Talents**

**14** "For it is just like a man who was *about* to take a journey, and he called his servants together and entrusted them with his possessions. **15** To one he gave five [b]talents, to another, two, and to another, one, each according to his own ability; and then he went on his journey.

**16** The one who had received the five talents went at once and traded with them, and he [made a profit and] gained five more. **17** Likewise the one who had two [made a profit and] gained two more. **18** But the one who had received the one went and dug *a hole* in the ground and hid his master's money.

**19** "Now after a long time the master of those servants returned and settled accounts with them. **20** And the one who had received the five talents came and brought him five more, saying, 'Master, you entrusted to me five talents. See, I have [made a profit and] gained five more talents.' **21** His master said to him, 'Well done, good and faithful servant. You have been faithful *and* trustworthy over a little, I will put you in charge of many things; share in the joy of your master.'

**22** "Also the one who had the two talents came forward, saying, 'Master, you entrusted two talents to me. See, I have [made a profit and] gained two more talents.' **23** His master said to him, 'Well done, good and faithful servant. You have been faithful *and* trustworthy over a little, I will put you in charge of many things; share in the joy of your master.'

**24** "The one who had received one talent also came forward, saying, 'Master, I knew you to be a harsh *and* demanding man, reaping [the harvest] where you did not sow and gathering where you did not scatter *seed*. **25** So I was afraid [to lose the talent], and I went and hid your talent in the ground. See, you have what is your own.'

**26** "But his master answered him, 'You wicked, lazy servant, you knew that I reap [the harvest] where I did not sow and gather where I did not scatter *seed*. **27** Then you ought to have put my money with the bankers, and at my return I would have received my *money* back with interest. **28** So take the talent away from him, and give it to the one who has the ten talents.'

**29** "For to everyone who has [and values his blessings and gifts from God, and has used them wisely], more will be given, and [he will be richly supplied so that] he will have an abundance; but from the one who does not have [because he has ignored or disregarded his blessings and gifts from God], even what he does have will be taken away. **30** And throw out the worthless servant into the outer darkness; in that place [of grief and torment] there will be weeping [over sorrow and pain] and grinding of teeth [over distress and anger]" ~Mt 25:15--28

This bible lesson is very instructive and plain. I hope you got the lesson internalised.

If you want your income to grow you have to take the responsibility to increase your capacity.

It's not Just school, it is personal development.

If Your capacity is 20k, and you are given 10M, you will reduce to 20k conversely it is so.

It's not money first, it is capacity. You consciously develop yourself.

Every business you want to do, increase your capacity. Even in your career, as a career person. God doesn't give you the size of capacity you have. You must be determined to increase your capacity. You must take the extra courses, read the books, take the classes, attend the seminars, take more degrees, watch those educative YouTube videos etc


You can't get more money when your capacity has not grown. Don't desire a big office without having the capacity for that office. You will run aground, And become envious of others who have built capacity and are successful.


It's not how much that is given to you, but the capacity you have. If you have handled money before and can't account for it, then your capacity is low. Have ingenuity, innovation, creativity, applicable knowledge etç

## Chapter 9

Practical steps to increase your income

1. Consult the Holy Spirit

"**9** but just as it is written [in Scripture],

"Things which the eye has not seen and the ear has not heard,

And which have not entered the heart of man,

All that God has prepared for those who love Him [who hold Him in affectionate reverence, who obey Him, and who gratefully recognize the benefits that He has bestowed]."

**10** For God has unveiled them *and* revealed *them* to us through the [Holy] Spirit; for the Spirit searches all things [diligently], even [sounding and measuring] the [profound] depths of God [the divine counsels and things far beyond human understanding]. **11** For what person knows the thoughts and motives of a man except the man's spirit within him? So also no one knows the *thoughts* of God except the Spirit of God. **12** Now we have received, not the spirit of the world, but the [Holy] Spirit who is from God, so that we may know *and* understand the [wonderful] things freely given to us by God." ~ 1Cor2: 9--12

If you want to beat unbelievers, always consult the Holy Spirit regularly.

Ask the Holy Spirit on how to solve your challenges including business, family, academics

2. Learn to set out time in a quiet place. "**16** So Daniel went in and asked the king to appoint a date *and* give him time, so

that he might reveal to the king the interpretation *of the dream.*" ~ Daniel 2:16.

Learn to have quiet time.

"18. Come now, and let us reason together,"

Says the Lord.

"Though your sins are like scarlet,

They shall be as white as snow;

Though they are red like crimson,

They shall be like wool." ~ Isaiah 1:18.

**Wealth is man's capacity to think. Don't think of problems, think of solutions.**

"**8** Finally, [b]believers, whatever is true, whatever is honorable *and* worthy of respect, whatever is right *and* confirmed by God's word, whatever is pure *and* wholesome, whatever is lovely *and* brings peace, whatever is admirable *and* of good repute; if there is any excellence, if there is anything worthy of praise, think *continually* on these things [center your mind on them, and implant them in your heart]" ~ Philippians 4:8

3. Seek supernatural counsel from the Holy Spirit "Trust in *and* rely confidently on the Lord with all your heart

And do not rely on your own insight *or* understanding." ~ Proverbs 3:5.

So you know it's a sign of arrogance if you don't pray to God to ask him something.

One way to consult the Holy Spirit is to sing worship songs and pray in tongues

4. Be creative. Creativity is the search for a solution. Creative people are very curious. Never take any assignment and leave it the way they gave you.

5. Be studious

The difference between your today and tomorrow, poverty and riches is information.

You can't use the wrong knowledge to get the right result.

"**2** in the first year of his reign, I, Daniel, understood from the books the number of years which, according to the word of the Lord to Jeremiah the prophet, must pass before the desolations [which had been] pronounced on Jerusalem would end; and it was seventy years." ~ Daniel 9:2

In conclusion, an increase of income should be the desire of progressive individuals who want more out of life.

This means you must choose to be more than ordinary and just exist here on earth.

Imagine how much more impact you could make in the life of your family, relatives, friends and society at large.

Until you become more, you cant have more.

And to have more means you must align with the principles laid herewith in this book.

I want to hear your story after taking these action steps to step up your income and become great in society.

I await celebrating your impact in this lifetime. Go on and become great!

All rights reserved Efezino Akpotu

Contact information:

Email: efeheritage@yahoo.com

Phone: 08080224596 (WhatsApp Also)

www.ingramcontent.com/pod-product-compliance
Lightning Source LLC
Chambersburg PA
CBHW060440220526
45465CB00008B/3216